MSC

HABITATS

POLAR REGIONS

NIGEL BONNER

Wayland

HABITATS

Coasts

Deserts

Forests

Grasslands

Islands

Mountains

Polar Regions

Rivers and Lakes

Seas and Oceans

Wetlands

Cover: Penguins on an ice floe in Antarctica.
Title page: Tourists explore icebergs floating in the Southern Ocean.
Contents page: Polar bears hunting on the Arctic ice.

Series editor: Rosemary Ashley
Book editor: Paul Bennett
Series designer: Malcolm Walker

First published in 1995 by
Wayland (Publishers) Limited
61 Western Road, Hove
East Sussex, BN3 1JD, England

British Library Cataloguing in Publication Data
Bonner, Nigel
    Polar Regions. - (Habitats series)
    I. Title   II. Series
    919.8

ISBN 0-7502-1488-0

Typeset by Kudos Editorial and Design Services
Printed and bound in Italy by L.E.G.O. S.p.A., Vicenza, Italy

CONTENTS

1. THE ENDS OF THE EARTH

Every day, as day breaks or night falls, we are reminded that the earth is spinning on its axis as it circles the sun. The Poles mark the farthest north and the farthest south points on this axis. Around the Poles, in the polar regions, the curve of the earth's surface means that the sun's rays strike the earth at a slant, so that the radiation from the sun is spread out over a greater area than it is in the tropics, closer to the equator. In addition, at the Poles the sunlight and heat has to pass through a greater thickness of atmosphere and this soaks up much of the heat. The result of this is that the polar regions are cold areas, covered with snow and ice.

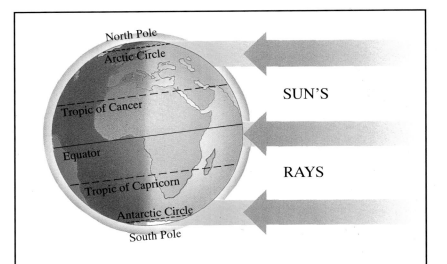

North Pole
Arctic Circle
Tropic of Cancer
Equator
Tropic of Capricorn
Antarctic Circle
South Pole

SUN'S

RAYS

Polar light and heat
Radiation from the sun, bringing light and heat energy to the earth, is spread over a much wider area at the Poles than it is within the tropics. The rays have a longer passage through the atmosphere at the Poles and this absorbs much of the heat, making the Poles colder.

Left The international research base at the South Pole. The South Pole is in the Antarctic.

The midnight sun in Finland, a country that borders the Arctic Ocean. During the Arctic summer months, the sun shines continuously on at least one day a year north of the Arctic Circle.

The region around the North Pole is called the Arctic. This gets its name from a Greek word meaning 'bear' because the star constellation of the Great Bear lies above the North Pole. The South Pole is in the region called the Antarctic, a name that means 'opposite the Arctic'.

A magnetic pole lies near each of the geographic Poles, but they are always moving around the polar regions. This means that we must keep adjusting our compass bearings, which are magnetic, to find true north.

The axis of the earth is not upright; it is tilted slightly. Because of this tilting, the Poles have opposite seasons. For example, when it is summer in the Arctic it is winter in the Antarctic. In summer, this tilting makes one of the polar regions lean towards the sun giving it long days, while in winter, when the tilt means the region leans away from the sun, the days are very short. At the Poles themselves, there is only one 'day' and one 'night' in the whole year. Day lasts from spring to autumn when the sun shines continuously, and 'night' lasts for the whole winter, when the sun sets and does not rise again until the following spring.

Limits of the polar regions

On a globe there are circles marked around the Poles which are called the Arctic Circle and the Antarctic Circle. These imaginary lines mark the limits of the polar regions and are marked at 66½ degrees north and south latitude. But the Polar Circles are not considered to make very good limits for what we generally regard as the polar regions. This is because the areas between these two circles do not always match the very cold conditions we expect to find within the polar regions. For example, northern Norway lies north of the Arctic Circle, but there are trees and farms there; while the South Shetland Islands (south of the equator) are far north of the Antarctic Circle, but there are no trees there and the average daily temperature rarely rises above freezing.

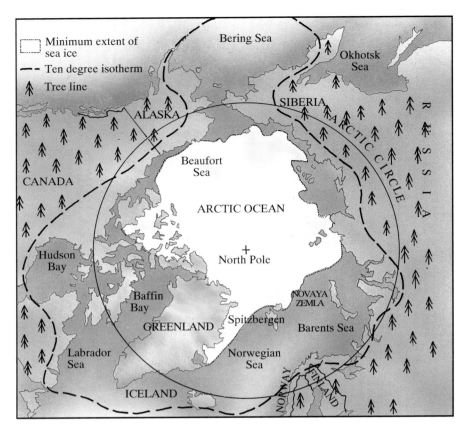

Map showing the Arctic Circle and ten degree isotherm. Much of the Arctic Ocean and Greenland are covered permanently by ice. No full-sized trees will grow north of the tree line.

Because we think of the polar regions as being the cold parts of the earth, measuring the temperature is a better way of finding their limits. A line joining all the places where the average maximum temperature of the warmest month is 10°C (known as the ten degree isotherm) is often used to define the polar regions. In the northern hemisphere, the ten degree isotherm line dips below the Arctic Circle to include southern Greenland and the north of Labrador in Canada, but rises above it in northern Norway and Russia. The ten degree isotherm corresponds quite closely with the northern limits at which forests will grow, known as the tree line.

In the southern hemisphere, the Antarctic continent is surrounded by water. Here, the limit is imagined at the northern boundary of cold Antarctic water, known as the Antarctic convergence (see page 8). This includes not only the Antarctic continent, but also islands, such as South Georgia.

Contrasts – land and sea

Although the Arctic and Antarctic are both cold regions, they have a very different geography. The Arctic consists of a shallow sea, the Arctic Ocean, most of which is covered with permanent pack ice, and which is surrounded

Right Map of the Antarctic. The Antarctic continent (Antarctica) takes up most of the area inside the Antarctic Circle.

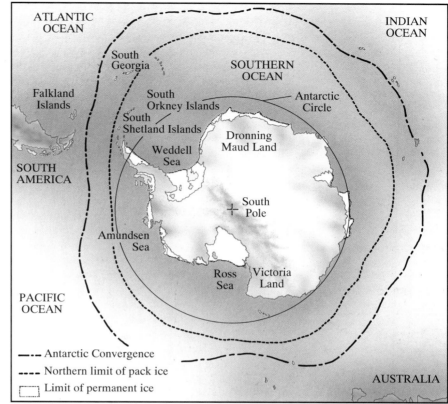

by the northern margins of the continents of Europe, Asia and North America. The Arctic Ocean is connected to the Pacific Ocean at the Bering Strait, between Alaska (USA) and Siberia (Russia), and to the North Atlantic by the much wider Norwegian Sea, between Norway and Greenland.

Greenland is the largest of a number of islands in the Arctic Ocean. Other Arctic islands are Baffin Island, off Canada; Novaya Zemlya, off Russia; and Spitzbergen north of Norway.

Spectacular and beautiful ice formations can be found in the Arctic.

The Antarctic is quite different. Antarctica is the fifth largest continent in the world, almost twice as big as Australia or the size of Europe and the USA put together. It makes up a tenth of the world's land surface. Antarctica is almost completely covered by a layer of ice with an average thickness of 2,000 kilometres. This great weight of ice presses the Antarctic continent down so that more than half of the underlying rock lies below sea-level. Even so, Antarctica is the highest of all the continents, with an average height three times that of the other continents.

This large, ice-covered continent is surrounded by the Southern Ocean. At the northern boundary of the Southern Ocean, a layer of very cold sea water, which is being blown away from the Antarctic by polar winds, suddenly dips under the warmer water north of it. This meeting of cold and warmer water is called the Antarctic convergence.

In the Southern Ocean there are several island groups, for example, the South Shetland Islands and the South Orkney Islands, so-called because they are at about the same southern latitude as the northern latitude of the Orkney and Shetland islands.

The Southern Ocean acts as a cold barrier around Antarctica, which has meant that there are far fewer different animals and plants in the Antarctic than in the Arctic.

Drifting continents – the origin of Antarctica

Antarctica was not always in the same place as it is now: about 200 million years ago, long before the dinosaurs, all the earth's continents were grouped together. Later, a southern super-continent, Gondwana, moved away and began to split up. What was to become South America drifted north near to North America, while a large area of land, Africa, moved to collide with the piece that was to become Europe. Another area, India, hit Asia and pushed up the great mountain range, the Himalayas. Madagascar, Australia and New Zealand drifted off separately, while Antarctica drifted towards the South Pole.

Previously, Antarctica had been covered with lush tropical forests, but at its polar position it received less warmth from the sun so it gradually began to cool. Ice formed and this reflected back a lot of the sun's heat and it got even colder. The reptiles, amphibians, trees and tree ferns have all gone from the Antarctic, but their fossils can be found today.

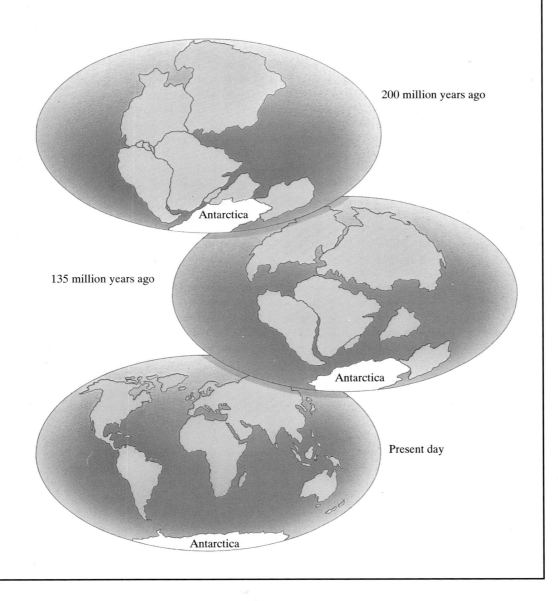

200 million years ago

Antarctica

135 million years ago

Antarctica

Present day

Antarctica

2. LANDS AND SEAS OF ICE

When water becomes cold enough, it turns to a solid we know as ice. When water vapour (a gas) freezes up in the clouds, it forms snowflakes. Snowflakes are complex crystals of ice. The shape and size of the snowflakes depend on the height and temperature at which they were formed, but they always show a pattern of six 'arms' or sides.

Snow is the origin of all the ice in the polar regions. Water vapour from the oceans in warmer parts of

Above   A glacier flows slowly down a Norwegian mountain. As it meets the Arctic Ocean, pieces break off to form icebergs.

Above   A large, flat-topped iceberg floats majestically in the chilly Arctic Ocean. Icebergs can tower hundreds of metres above the ocean's surface.

Ice as a record of global pollution

The ice that forms over Antarctica builds up in layers, each corresponding to one year's snowfall. Scientists can drill out cores of the ice and, by counting down from the top, can accurately date each layer. These layers can be melted and the water from them can be analysed for pollutants, such as radioactive substances released by atomic explosions, that were present in the air when the snow fell.

Recent studies have shown that the concentrations of lead in ice have become lower since the introduction of lead-free motor fuel. Antarctic ice-core studies can help us to keep a check on pollution levels caused by motor vehicles and industry thousands of kilometres away.

A scientist holds a core of ice drilled from the Antarctic ice-cap. The ice will be studied for evidence of pollutants.

the world rises into the sky. The snow formed from this vapour falls and settles over the poles and does not melt because it is so cold. Gradually, the weight of all the snow squeezes the crystals into solid ice. Although the amount of snowfall over the poles is quite low, the snow keeps building up in layers to form an ice-cap. The Antarctic has the largest ice-cap in the world, with about 90 per cent of all the world's ice, equivalent to some 70 per cent of all the earth's fresh water. The weight of the accumulating ice causes it to flow slowly (between 1 and 10 metres per year) towards the edges of the continent.

When this sheet of slowly-moving ice finally reaches the sea, it floats out as an ice-shelf, which eventually breaks off to form flat-topped tabular icebergs. Some of these may be more than a hundred kilometres long.

When the ice flows down a steep slope it forms a glacier. If a glacier then reaches the sea, it forms small, irregular icebergs. Most Arctic icebergs are of this type.

Ice and its effects on the land

Where glaciers flow down a valley, the ice has a great effect on the underlying surface. The slowly moving ice pulls small fragments of rock from the rock surface, while larger pieces of rock become trapped in the moving ice, making deep scratches in the land. Over the centuries, this glacial action produces a characteristic landscape that is revealed when the ice retreats.

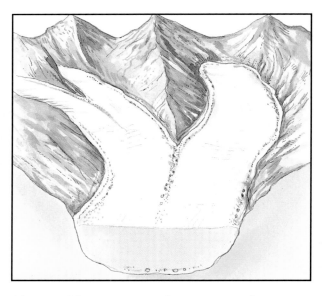

Above   Glaciers cut into the mountainsides leaving valleys in the shape of a letter U.

Above   Needle-shaped mountain peaks are evidence of the repeated freezing and thawing of water.

In the summer, the sea ice breaks up around the Antarctic continent. In the winter, the pack ice will extend far beyond the Antarctic Circle.

Antarctica – the expanding and shrinking continent

The Antarctic continent covers about 14 million sq km. However, each autumn as the sea freezes around its shore, the ice surface of Antarctica increases in size. The expansion of the pack ice begins about March and the frozen surface spreads out at more than 4 km per day, until by September some 20 million sq km of sea is covered. As summer comes again, the pack ice breaks up and melts, except in a few places. By the end of February, it has been reduced to only 4 million sq km. Seen from a satellite, the effect of this is that the Antarctic continent seems to expand and shrink each year as the ice advances and recedes.

Ice has another way of breaking down rock. When water freezes it expands slightly. Although this expansion is small, it is very powerful. Have you ever had a burst pipe in your home in the winter? This is caused by the water in the pipe freezing. In polar regions, if water gets into a crack in a rock, when it freezes it splits the rock. During a polar summer, repeated freezing and thawing of water, which can occur over many days, will soon break down rocks. You can tell which mountains have been exposed to this process by their characteristic needle-shaped peaks.

Sea ice

Besides icebergs, which come from ice sheets or glaciers on land, the sea surface itself can freeze to form sea ice. As the temperature falls at the end of the polar summer, small crystals of ice form on the surface of the sea, giving it an oily appearance. These join together and make a thin sheet which the wind and waves break up into pancake ice. The pancake ice thickens until large chunks of it are floating in the sea. This is pack ice. Eventually, the floes of the pack ice join together until no open water can be seen, except where the wind or currents of water keep an area of sea free of ice. An area of open water in an otherwise icy sea is called a lead or polynya.

Most Antarctic pack ice melts each spring, but in the Arctic Ocean the pack ice lasts for many years, growing thicker and building up into huge pressure ridges, forced up by the wind and currents.

Strange, honeycomb patterns in the permafrost of the Russian Arctic.

Ice and climate

Not only does the amount of ice show that the polar regions have a cold climate, but it also makes the climate colder. The shining white surface of the ice reflects the sun's heat, so the polar regions cannot absorb as much warmth from the sun as regions without ice. This causes strange extremes – people unloading cargo on an ice shelf in the summer may take off their shirts and get sunburn while the air temperature is a chilly minus 10°C, for example.

Where there is soil in polar regions, it is often permanently frozen beneath the surface. This is called permafrost. In the Arctic summer, the surface of the soil thaws and vegetation may grow well. But if the surface cover is disturbed, for example, when buildings are erected, the permafrost may melt, causing the buildings to tilt or sink. When the oil pipelines in Alaska were built, it was necessary to fit special radiators to the supports of the pipes. These radiators transmitted 'cold' from the air down to the foundations in the permafrost, so that the pipes did not bend and break.

Where the soil is exposed, the ground may develop strange markings, often of a honeycomb pattern, or it has parallel ridges with exposed stones. This patterned ground is caused by the expansion and contraction of the soil water as it freezes and thaws repeatedly. Little vegetation can grow on the disturbed area of soil and stones.

Pingos are strange, steep-sided mounds found in many Arctic areas. A pingo contains a core of ice and is formed when a small lake over the permafrost drains away and freezes in the underlying mud. As the ice expands, it is squeezed out of the mud to form the bulb of ice at the centre of the pingo. Pingos can rise 10 metres or more above the surface of the land.

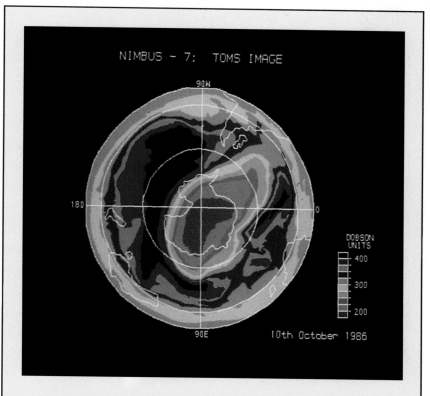

In the early 1980s, a 'hole' was found in the protective ozone layer high above Antarctica. Scientists use pictures like this to show how the ozone layer is changing.

The ozone 'hole'

A layer of ozone high up in the atmosphere (in the stratosphere) protects us from the harmful effects of the sun's ultraviolet radiation. We now know this ozone layer has been damaged, largely by chemicals called chlorofluorocarbons (CFCs), developed for use in refrigerators and aerosols. This damage was first seen in the Antarctic, where the thinning of the ozone layer – it is not really a hole – is most apparent.

CFCs are complex chemicals containing chlorine. When the CFCs escape into the stratosphere, the chlorine attacks the ozone, which is broken down to oxygen. The oxygen does not absorb the harmful ultraviolet rays, which cause skin cancer, and so the ozone layer does not provide its original protection. There is now an international agreement to limit and eventually end the production and use of CFCs.

3. LIFE IN POLAR REGIONS

If you visit the Arctic tundra (the treeless plains of Arctic Europe, Asia and North America) during the short northern summer, you might be surprised by the colourful, flower-filled meadows that you see there. During the long winter, the plants die back, or exist as seeds. All polar plants have to be very hardy, but the cold is not the main problem for them. Plants can survive very low temperatures, but they cannot grow without water for their roots to take up. This means that they have to have shallow roots to take advantage of the moisture in the thin layer of soil that thaws when spring arrives.

Tundra plants hug the ground to avoid the drying winds and to take advantage of the way the sun's radiation warms the ground surface even when the air temperature is below freezing. One of the most remarkable tundra plants is the Arctic willow. This is a dwarf tree, which may have branches more than 5 metres in length, but never rises much more than 10 centimetres from the ground.

Many colourful, low-growing plants manage to survive in the harsh climate of the Arctic tundra.

The Antarctic contrasts greatly with the Arctic. In Greenland alone you can find more than 500 flowering plants, but in the Antarctic there are only two – a small grass and a plant called *Colobanthus* (it has no common name). The lack of flowering plants in the Antarctic is due to its isolation. The Arctic tundras are connected to temperate, plant-rich lands and temperate plants have been able to adapt to Arctic conditions and colonize the tundra. The Southern Ocean has prevented most plants from reaching the Antarctic. Perhaps the seeds of the grass and *Colobanthus* which do exist there were brought to the Antarctic on birds' feathers.

But in both polar regions there are many mosses and lichens, and in some places these are the only plants that will grow. In the severest conditions in the Antarctic, the only plant life is a lichen that actually grows inside tiny cracks in the rocks.

Keeping alive in the cold

Like plants, animals have to keep themselves from freezing if they are to stay alive. Mini-beasts have the biggest problems. Some of them, such as mites and springtails, avoid freezing by producing a kind of antifreeze in their blood, like the liquid we put into a car's radiator in cold weather. Often these tiny

These are the two flowering plants that can be found in Antarctica – a small grass (top) and a low-growing plant called *Colobanthus*.

A lemming scampers beneath the melting tundra snow. It has woken from its deep winter sleep (hibernation) and is looking for food.

animals are black or very dark brown, so that they can absorb the sun's radiation and warm up quickly.

Warm-blooded animals must keep warm or they will die of cold. Polar mammals and birds have thick fur or feather coats, which trap a layer of warm air near their skins. Some have a layer of fat or blubber under their skin, which is a good insulator. This prevents heat from escaping from their bodies.

Polar animals also need a lot of food, to provide the energy to keep them warm. During the winter when food is hard to find, some tundra animals, such as lemmings, fall into a special deep sleep called hibernation and live on the reserves of food they have in their bodies in the form of fat.

Food chains

In the Arctic where there is quite a lot of vegetation, there are plant-eating animals, or herbivores, such as musk-oxen and Arctic hares. These herbivores are the food of flesh-eaters (carnivores), such as polar bears, wolves or Arctic foxes. These form a food chain. Without the carnivores, the herbivores might eat all the plants and then starve. As elsewhere, carnivores are essential to preserve the balance of nature in the Arctic.

Mini-beasts have similar relationships. Greenfly suck the sap of plants and ladybirds feed on the greenfly. Some mini-beasts attack much larger animals.

Many mosquitoes and blackflies breed in the pools of the tundra and these suck the blood of birds and mammals.

In contrast, the Antarctic has no large land animals. Because there is so little vegetation, the largest herbivores are mini-beasts. Without large herbivores there can be no large carnivores. A food chain on land in the Antarctic might consist of a herbivore mite, feeding on fungi and being fed on by a carnivore mite. There are no biting flies in the Antarctic, so the only mammals on land there, the birds and seals, are not plagued by them.

Above   Mosquitoes breed in the tundra pools. This one is using its biting mouthparts to suck the blood of a human.

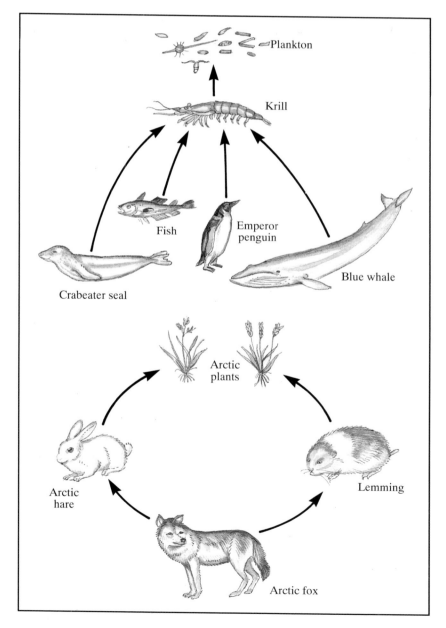

The Arctic 'woolly bear'
One of the longest-lived Arctic insects is the caterpillar of a moth. This 'woolly bear' lives on Arctic willow leaves, but it can eat only the young, tender leaves. The caterpillar emerges from hibernation in the spring and starts eating the willow leaves as they unfold. But as summer approaches, the leaves get too bitter to eat and so the caterpillar crawls away to hibernate again, although summer is not over. Next year it emerges again to eat the next season's crop of young leaves.

This can go on for twelve years before the caterpillar finally spins a cocoon, carefully angled to get the best exposure to the sun, and then turns into a moth. The moths live for only a few days before mating and laying their eggs on the willow.

Left   Some simple polar food chains. In the Southern Ocean, tiny plankton are fed on by krill, which in turn are food for a great many different creatures. In the Arctic tundra, plant-eating animals are food for meat-eaters.

A killer whale comes close to the shore hoping to catch a king penguin.

Life in polar seas

In polar regions the sea is very often warmer than the air. Sea water cannot get colder than minus 1.8°C, at which point it freezes, and this is much warmer than even the air temperature in the Antarctic summer. This means that life can flourish in polar seas just as well as it does in other cold seas. Polar seas are rich in many different kinds of life.

All marine life depends on plankton, the tiny plants and animals that float in the water. The nutrient salts that the plankton need to survive are brought to the polar oceans by currents from warmer oceans. During the long summer days, the plankton grow very quickly. Animal plankton graze on the plant plankton and these in turn provide food for larger animals, such as fish, seals and whales. Some of these larger animals are themselves fed on by other carnivores, and the food chain becomes a complicated food web.

Seals, walruses, polar bears and penguins

Seals and walruses are especially common in polar regions. Seals feed

From the smallest to the biggest

Whales are mammals that live in the sea and have their calves there. The rich food in cold polar waters attracts whales during the summer. Some whales, such as the blue whale, have developed a special method for filtering out plankton from the sea. Hanging down from the blue whale's upper jaw are a series of 'plates' fringed with fine hairs. The whale takes a huge mouthful of water containing plankton and then closes its mouth and strains the water out through the plates. The plankton are caught on the hairs and the whale swallows them.

Blue whales are the largest animals that have ever lived, much larger than dinosaurs. A 30 metre blue whale weighs about 150 tonnes and needs to catch between 4.5 and 6 million krill every day to satisfy its hunger. Remarkably, it can do this in only about eighty gulps, so large is its mouth and so abundant the krill.

on fish, squid or plankton, while walruses find their food on the floor of shallow seas, feeding on clams, cockles and other animals. Seals spend most of their time in the water and their blubber keeps them warm. Polar seals mostly come out on to the ice to have their young. The mother seal feeds her pup on the rich milk she produces for a very short period – the hooded seal pup is weaned at only four days old, for example.

Polar bears live only in the Arctic. They eat fish but feed mainly on seals which they catch by waiting for them at breathing holes in the ice. Polar bears are closely related to grizzly bears, but are larger. Their thick, white coats, with a layer of blubber beneath, keep them warm. The mother polar bear gives birth to her cubs, usually two, during the winter. She keeps them in the den she has hollowed out in a snow bank until spring, feeding them on her milk.

Penguins are found in the Antarctic. Penguins are birds that have lost the power to fly. Their wings have turned into flippers, with which they 'fly' through the water. Their bodies are covered with small, oily feathers that overlap like the tiles on a roof and cover a layer of down that stays dry no matter how long the penguins have been in the water.

Above After feeding, a mother seal returns to its pup through a hole in the ice. Polar seals give birth to their pups on the ice.

Left Polar bears lumber across the Arctic ice looking for seals. They are at home in the icy water and will swim many kilometres to find new hunting grounds.

An emperor penguin chick sits on its parent's feet. Male emperor penguins have a special pouch for keeping the egg warm while the female goes to feed in the Antarctic Ocean.

Most penguins make nests of small pebbles in which they lay two eggs, but the largest penguin, the emperor penguin, does not make a nest at all. Instead, the female lays an egg on the ice in the middle of winter. The male immediately scoops it up on to his feet and lowers a flap of skin over it, so that his body can keep the egg warm until it hatches. Then both parents busy themselves bringing back small fish to feed the single chick. There is not enough room for two eggs on the male's feet, so the female emperor penguin lays only one.

4. POLAR RESOURCES

Resources are those things found in nature which humans need as raw materials for their industries, or as fuels or food. The polar regions have their share of the world's natural resources.

Arctic minerals

We obtain many minerals from the Arctic. There are deposits of iron and tin ore in Arctic Russia, and lead is found in west Greenland and Arctic Canada. Gold was once found in the Yukon Valley, in Canada, and there are still gold mines in Arctic Russia. On the island of Spitzbergen, coal is mined by a Russian company.

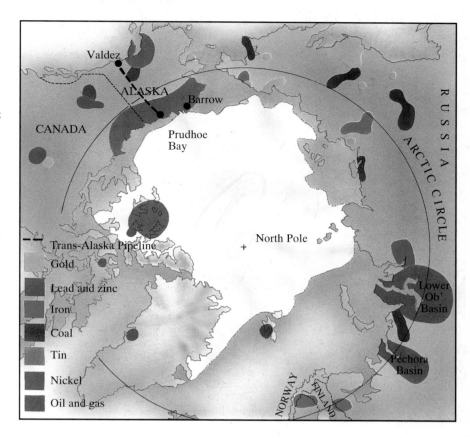

Valdez
ALASKA
Barrow
CANADA
Prudhoe Bay
North Pole
RUSSIA
ARCTIC CIRCLE
Lower Ob' Basin
Pechora Basin
NORWAY
FINLAND

- - - Trans-Alaska Pipeline
Gold
Lead and zinc
Iron
Coal
Tin
Nickel
Oil and gas

Above Map showing the resources that can be found in the Arctic.

Left The Trans-Alaska Pipeline carries oil across the Alaskan tundra. In places, the pipeline is raised up high to allow migrating reindeer to pass.

23

An off-shore drill rig operates in the shallow waters of the Beaufort Sea. Rich reserves of oil and gas are found off Alaska and Arctic Canada.

Very large reserves of the earth's resources of oil and natural gas are found in the Arctic. Russia's oil and gas reserves are mostly beneath the land in the basins of the Ob' and Pechora Rivers. In Alaska and Arctic Canada, much of the oil and gas occurs beneath the shallow waters of the Beaufort Sea. The Beaufort Sea is covered with very heavy pack ice for much of the year, which presents the oil engineers with problems in drilling their wells to reach it. Drill ships, which are used in the North Sea, are in danger of being crushed by the ice. To avoid this, the engineers first make artificial islands of millions of tonnes of gravel dredged up from the mouths of the rivers and then build their drilling rigs on these islands.

A huge pipe, the Trans-Alaska Pipeline, carries the oil from where it is drilled, across the tundra and through the forests, until it reaches an ice-free port from where it can be carried by tankers to be used by the rest of the world.

Antarctic minerals

Because nearly all of the Antarctic continent is covered with a thick layer of ice, no techniques exist at present for finding or extracting minerals. Many people feel that the Antarctic should be left to the wildlife and that it is too beautiful to risk starting to mine minerals there. In 1991, all the nations with interests in the Antarctic agreed to forbid exploration for Antarctic minerals. But they agreed, too, that scientific research could be carried out there.

A worker struggles with a hose at a gas drilling rig on the Yamal Peninsula in Russia's Siberia.

Sealing and whaling

Inuit people – the native people from North America or Greenland – had always hunted seals and whales for food, fuel and clothing. Four hundred years ago, European fishermen started to hunt seals around Newfoundland for the oil that could be extracted from their blubber. These were harp seals that spent most of the year feeding in Arctic waters, but came to the drifting pack ice off Newfoundland to breed in the spring. Millions of harp seals were killed in the last century for oil, leather and food.

After the Second World War (1939–45), although hunting the seals for their oil was still important, what the hunters were really after were the pups, for their beautiful white fur from which fashionable clothes were made. In the 1980s, many people thought it was wrong to kill seal pups and in 1983 the European Economic Community (EEC) banned the import of pup skins. As the skins could not then be sold in Europe, the industry became much less profitable and there is little commercial hunting carried out today.

A southern right whale breaks the surface in the krill-rich waters of the Antarctic Ocean. After the Second World War, many species of whale were hunted near to extinction.

Although whales have been hunted in every ocean of the world, the Antarctic was the most important area. Antarctic whaling started in 1904 and soon expanded because of the huge numbers of whales to be found there. After the Second World War, when there were great shortages of fat and oil in Europe and elsewhere, whale oil became a very valuable resource. It was used as cooking oil or turned into margarine and soap. Unfortunately, the whalers killed far too many whales and reduced their populations severely, though fortunately no whale species became extinct. In 1987, an agreement was made to stop commercial whaling in the Antarctic, and in 1994 the Antarctica waters were declared a reserve for all whales.

An abandoned whaling station on the South Atlantic island of South Georgia. Whalers would use this station to process the whales they caught for oil.

Fisheries

Fish are important polar resources. Some of the fish caught in Arctic waters are familiar to us, such as cod, haddock and herring. Others, such as capelin, are not used directly to feed humans, but are processed into oil and fish-meal, which is then fed to chickens. Modern developments in fishing techniques,

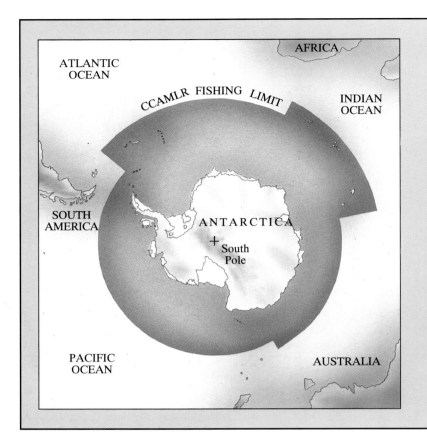

ATLANTIC OCEAN

AFRICA

CCAMLR FISHING LIMIT

INDIAN OCEAN

SOUTH AMERICA

ANTARCTICA

+ South Pole

PACIFIC OCEAN

AUSTRALIA

Protection of Antarctic fish

Commercial fishing started in the Antarctic in the 1960s. None of the fish caught there are familiar to us, but many can be used to produce fillets or fish fingers. Krill is also caught to make krill-meal, which is used for feeding chickens or farmed fish. Russian and Polish fishing boats started fishing, but too many fish were caught and stocks declined. The Antarctic fishing nations and others with an interest in the Antarctic met in 1980 and agreed to a treaty – the Convention on the Conservation of Antarctic Marine Living Resources (CCAMLR) – that would regulate fishing in the Antarctic. The convention includes all living things in the sea and sea birds. All catches of fish are controlled to ensure that the waters are not over-fished.

The CCAMLR fishing limit ensures that enough fish are left for seals and penguins to catch.

particularly electronic fish finders, that enable the fishermen to locate shoals of fish accurately, have meant that much larger amounts of fish are now being caught. There are fears today that more fish are being caught than can be replaced by natural breeding and growth. Not only is the stock of fish available for human consumption being reduced, but also it is more difficult for the birds and seals that feed on fish to find their food.

A Russian research vessel passes the stern of a German fishing boat in Antarctic waters. Thanks to the CCAMLR treaty, fishing in the Southern Ocean is now controlled, allowing fish stocks to increase from dangerously over-fished levels.

5. PEOPLES OF THE POLES

In the countries bordering the Arctic Ocean, there are people who have adapted their life styles so that they can live in the harsh environment that they inhabit. The best known of these are the Inuit. The ancestors of these peoples originally came from Central Asia and moved to the shores of the polar ocean as the ice sheet retreated many thousands of years ago. Some of them crossed from Asia to North America across the Bering Straits. Sea levels were much lower then, and there was a land bridge which today is covered by sea.

In the north of Russia, the largest groups of these Arctic peoples are the Samoyed, the Yakut and the Chukchi. In Russia, these people were originally wandering reindeer herders, trappers and hunters, but now many live in towns and work in the local industry.

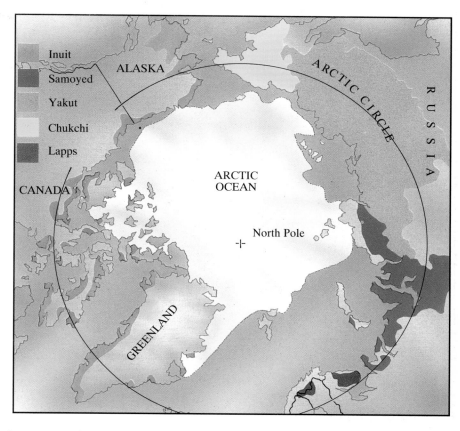

Above   Map showing where Arctic peoples can be found.

Left   An Inuit of north-west Greenland leaves on a hunting trip in his sealskin kayak.

29

An Inuit man stands outside his igloo. He is wearing clothing made from sealskins and fur and is holding a harpoon for catching seals.

The Inuit

The Inuit live mainly in Alaska, Arctic Canada and Greenland, and just a few live on the furthest eastern tip of Russia. In the past, although some Inuit hunted caribou (North American reindeer), the great majority were wholly dependent on the sea for their food. The men hunted seals and caught fish and sea birds. Some Alaskan groups even hunted bowhead whales. Seals were especially important, because they provided meat to eat, skins to make warm and waterproof clothing, and blubber. The blubber could be burnt in stone lamps to provide warmth and heat through the long winter darkness.

To keep warm, the Inuit dressed in clothing made not only of sealskin but also of fur. Different animals provided fur for different sorts of clothing. For example, the fur of a wolverine, a type of weasel, was used to line the hoods of

anoraks, because snow would not cling to it. The skins of Arctic hares, eider ducks and foxes combined warmth with lightness. Polar bear skin was exceedingly warm but tremendously heavy.

When they were hunting in boats, waterproof clothing was needed. The Greenlanders devised a combination suit of sealskin – hooded anorak (an Inuit word), mittens, trousers and boots, all in one piece. The wearer had to enter it through a hole in the chest, which was then closed tightly with draw strings.

The skin clothing devised by the Inuit was a very effective protection against the weather, but it required continual repair. The Inuit women were skilled at maintaining the clothing, using bone needles and thread made from the sinews of animals to repair the skins they wore.

Most Inuit lived entirely on meat and fish that contained a very high proportion of fat. Although we consider fat to be unhealthy, it was a healthy diet for them as they needed the energy from the fat to keep them warm.

As recently as a hundred years ago, some Inuit families were living almost untouched by modern civilization. Their life was not simple, however. They could endure the harsh Arctic environment only because their tools, kayaks, harpoons and clothing were perfectly designed for the conditions they had to live in.

Today, Inuit and other Arctic peoples are abandoning their old life styles. Most Inuit now live in modern homes and go to the shops for their food and have access to health and social services. Many work on modern fishing boats or in the mines. In the summer, however, some return to their old ways – they go out hunting and build their traditional snow houses, or igloos.

Antarctic research stations

The Antarctic's isolation from other continents kept it uninhabited by people for thousands of years and, as a result, there are no native peoples in the Antarctic. It was only about two hundred years ago that explorers first set foot on the Antarctic continent. Today, however, many people make scientific expeditions to the Antarctic to study the weather, the wildlife, to make maps, or to investigate the structure of the ice and rocks. These people do not live in the Antarctic all the time. Most of them go there just for a few months in the summer, though some stay for the winter.

The research stations where the scientists and support staff such as engineers, cooks and radio operators live, contain quite large communities of people. The buildings forming the living area, laboratories and workshops are all well insulated to keep out the cold and to save the fuel that is used for heating them. Some stations are built on ice-shelves and can soon get covered in snow drifts. When a building becomes buried deep in the snow, it has to be abandoned and a new one is built.

Tourists in Antarctica

Many tourists now travel to the polar regions. In the Antarctic, tourist ships make voyages of two or three weeks in the summer to allow their passengers to see the beautiful scenery and wildlife of the Antarctic.

Equipment used by scientists in the Antarctic has to be specially constructed to withstand the harsh conditions.

Polar clothing today

The fur clothing once used by the Inuit is not easily obtained today. Instead, workers in the polar regions wear special fabrics to enable them to keep warm and comfortable and avoid frostbite.

Polar clothing must:
- keep the body warm, especially the fingers and toes;
- not allow perspiration to build up;
- allow free movement; and
- be comfortable, whatever the weather.

The 'layer' method, which involves wearing several layers of lightweight clothes, allows good ventilation as well as good insulation. A person working in the Antarctic might wear:
- cotton underwear;
- long-johns and a long-sleeved vest of synthetic material;
- a wool or synthetic shirt;
- fibre-pile trousers;
- a heavy-duty acrylic sweater;
- a fibre-pile jacket, with a high zip-up collar;

A party of tourists take to an inflatable boat for a trip around icebergs floating in the Southern Ocean. Nearby, their ship waits for them to return.

- a cotton windproof anorak and trousers;
- fine silk under-gloves, woollen or fibre-pile mittens and waxed cotton over-mittens with big cuffs;
- socks, felt inner boots and special outer boots ('mukluks' in Inuktitut, the language of the Inuit).

Polar transport

In the past the Inuit were famous for their use of sledges to travel over snow and ice. Their sledge dogs were essential companions. Bred from Arctic wolves, they were able to survive the severest conditions, by sleeping curled up in a snow-hole.

Today, dogs are hardly used. Motorized toboggans, or snow scooters, are now the preferred means of transport for Inuit hunters and trappers. This means that they have to purchase fuels and oils instead of catching seals to feed their dogs. Sledges are still used for moving large loads in the Antarctic, but they are towed by big tractors with very wide tracks that will not sink into the snow.

Modern vessels can penetrate pack ice with ease and take tourist parties to the North Pole. Aeroplanes equipped with skis instead of wheels can make survey flights and land on the snow. Helicopters are also used in the polar regions.

Lapps and their reindeer

Lapps are people who live in northern Norway, Sweden and Finland. Some are fishermen, hunters or trappers, but others live entirely from their reindeer herds. They wander about, leading the reindeer from one pasture to another, and feeding on their meat and milk. Traditionally, Lapps wear very colourful clothing. Sometimes they settle in one place for a length of time and live in tents made from reindeer skins, or in underground huts, roofed with turf.

A Lapp in traditional dress with his reindeer. The reindeer provide the basic needs of food, clothing and transport.

6. EXPLORATION OF THE POLES

The first Arctic explorers were the people who travelled north to occupy lands as the ice retreated. They are now represented by the Inuit, the Greenlanders and the Russian Arctic peoples. By around AD 870, seafaring Norsemen had visited the Kola Peninsula in Arctic Russia and Iceland, and established the first European colony. Later, in 985, the Norse navigator, Eric the Red, sailed to Greenland from Iceland, and established a colony there. The climate was warm in those days, and for a while this settlement flourished. But when the climate turned colder in the fourteenth and fifteenth centuries, the colonists fared less well, and a hundred years later they had all died or left the colony.

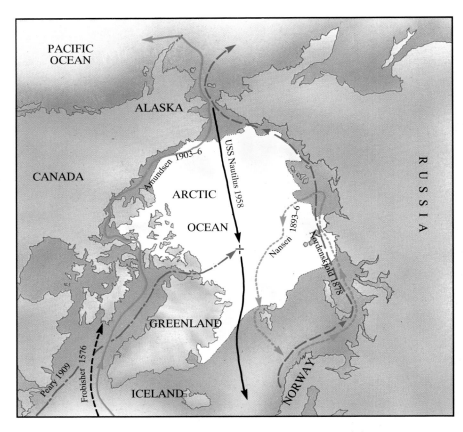

Map showing the routes taken by some of the explorers of the Arctic. It was not until 1909 that an American explorer, Robert Peary, claimed to have reached the point of the North Pole itself.

In the mid-1500s, English and Dutch sailors began to explore the Arctic as they searched for a north-east passage by sea around the north of Russia to China, but were defeated by the ice. Similarly, in 1576, Martin Frobisher searched for a north-west passage around northern North America and discovered Baffin Island. However, it was not until 1878 that the Swedish explorer, A E Nordenskjöld, completed the north-east passage. The Norwegian, Roald Amundsen, managed to complete the north-west passage, though it took him from 1903 to 1906!

Another Norwegian, Fridtjof Nansen, set off in 1893 in his immensely strong boat *Fram*, to try to reach the North Pole by drifting with the heavy pack ice. He missed the Pole, but got within 364 kilometres of it. It was not until 1909 that the American, Robert Peary, claimed to have reached the Pole itself, by travelling over the ice, though some people dispute this. In 1958, the US nuclear submarine USS *Nautilus* travelled under the ice and surfaced at the North Pole, the first ship to reach it. Now tourists can go to the Pole on Russian nuclear-powered ice-breakers.

The Antarctic

Though there is a Maori tradition that in about AD 650, Ui-te-Rangiora sailed in his canoe *Te Ivi-o-Atea* as far south as the frozen ocean, the first person to have crossed the Antarctic Circle and returned to leave a written record was Captain James Cook in HMS *Resolution* in January 1773.

Captain Cook's small ship was unable to penetrate the pack ice, so he never even sighted Antarctica. It was not until January 1820 that the Russian explorer, Thaddeus Bellingshausen, and the British naval officer, Edward Bransfield, first saw the coast of Antarctica. In November that year, the American seal hunter, Nathaniel Palmer, also sighted the coast.

In the next eighty years, because of the interest in hunting seals, and a general determination to discover more about the unknown continent, the governments of France, the USA and Britain sent out expeditions under the direction of Dumon d'Urville, Charles Wilkes and James Clark Ross respectively. They all added to the knowledge of the coastline.

The first scientific party to spend a winter on the Antarctic continent did so at Victoria Land in 1899. This British expedition, in the ship called the *Southern Cross*, was under the command of a Norwegian, Carsten Borchgrevink.

In 1902 Robert Scott, Edward Wilson and Ernest Shackleton attempted to travel overland to the South Pole. They got as far as 772 kilometres from the Pole before they were forced to turn back. Scott and Wilson, with three companions, tried again in 1911, hauling their sledges over the ice themselves. They reached the Pole on 18 January 1912, only to find

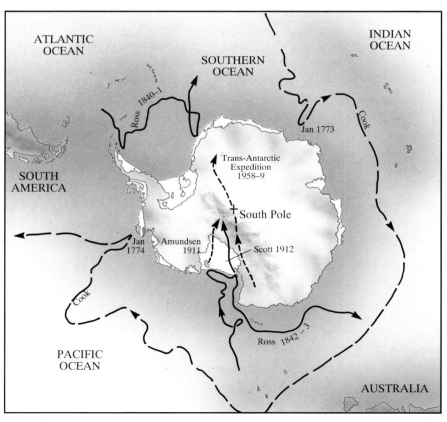

Map showing the routes taken by some famous Antarctic explorers.

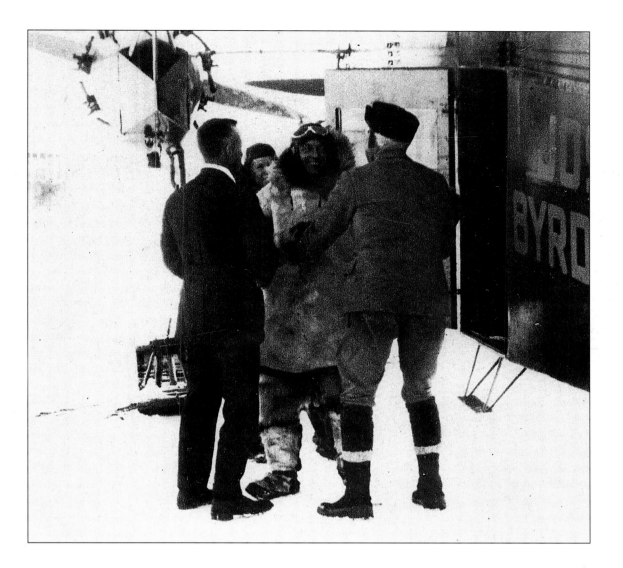

Richard Byrd is congratulated by Amundsen after his flight over the North Pole in 1926. Byrd later went on to fly over the South Pole.

that the Norwegian explorer, Roald Amundsen, had got there before them on 14 December 1911, having travelled quickly using dog sledges. Scott and his companions perished on the way back from the Pole.

The American, Richard Byrd, was the first to use aeroplanes for Antarctic exploration. Byrd flew over the Pole in November 1929. In 1946–7, the USA mounted 'Operation High Jump', which was the largest expedition ever to go to Antarctica, using 13 ships, 25 aircraft and more than 4,000 men.

The last big expedition was the joint British–New Zealand Trans-Antarctic Expedition in 1958, when a land crossing was made from the Weddell Sea to the Ross Sea, passing across the Pole.

By this time, several nations had set up scientific stations in the Antarctic. These included Argentina, Australia, Britain, Chile, France, Japan, New Zealand, Norway, South Africa, the Soviet Union and the USA. Scientists from all these countries, and many others, are continuing to explore the Antarctic and study everything from the breeding behaviour of penguins to the movement of the ice.

The modern exploration of Antarctica

Early explorers noted roughly the shape of Antarctica as they sailed past it, or laboriously towed their sledges over the ice. Mapping was made much easier by the use of aerial photography; maps could be prepared from photographs taken from an aircraft. This was what Richard Byrd did. Much more recently, it has been possible to make very accurate maps from photographs taken from a satellite high above the earth, so we now know precisely what the outline of the Antarctic is like.

But if we want to see the shape of the continent beneath its mantle of ice we have to use another method. This method is known as radio echo sounding. An aircraft flies over the ice and sends down a pulse of radar waves. This penetrates the ice and is reflected back from the underlying rock. A computer on the aircraft calculates the depth of the ice from the time it takes the pulse of radar waves to come back to the aircraft. From this a picture of the rock surface underneath the ice can be built up, and we see that Antarctica is not really one big continent, but a large one and several little ones, all joined by the ice-cap.

A scientific survey team crosses the icy wastes of Antarctica. The team's vehicles pull huge sledges which carry the equipment.

7. THE FUTURE OF THE POLAR REGIONS

The Inuit and other peoples went to the Arctic because it provided them with a homeland and a place where they could catch seals and the other animals that they lived on. Later, Europeans saw that they could exploit the Arctic – it was a possible trade route to China and they also found goods to trade, such as seal skins and walrus teeth for carving. In recent years, oil from the Arctic has become of very great importance to the economies of Canada and the USA.

At the other end of the world, almost as soon as Captain Cook first crossed the Antarctic Circle, sealers were visiting the islands off the Antarctic Peninsula to hunt fur seals and elephant seals for their skins and oil. Whaling started in 1904 and sixty years later nearly all the big whales had been killed.

It is natural that people should search for the world's resources wherever they can find them. Our modern society is founded on trade and manufacture, and both of these need natural resources to be successful. But we now know that it is important for us to protect the environment and use the resources wisely.

Whales being butchered on the deck of a factory ship. The overfishing of whales reduced the numbers of some species so drastically that they are now in danger of extinction.

The importance of conservation

Protecting the environment is the main task of conservation. This is quite a new idea, which started only about thirty years ago. Before then, there were laws that protected some fish or birds, but people had not realized that it was important to protect the environment as a whole. Now most people know that if we do not care for the environment we will all find it more difficult to live on the earth.

The polar regions are important for many reasons. All the ice that lies around the poles acts as a natural 'air conditioner' for the earth. If the ice were to melt, much more radiation would be absorbed from the sun instead of being reflected back, and the earth's climate would heat up and deserts would spread. Besides this, the melted ice would raise the level of the sea, so that much of the low-lying coastal parts of the world would be flooded.

The animals and plants of the polar regions are part of the great variety of life that exists on earth. We are now beginning to realize that all the plants and animals in the world form a 'web' that maintains life as we know it on earth. Losing plants or animals, whether they are from the Amazon forest or from the Arctic, weakens that web. Preserving all these different forms of life

Cleaning up an oil spill in Alaska. Both the Arctic and Antarctic need protection if they are not to be spoiled for ever.

Rubbish from a scientific station is being removed so that it will not spoil the fragile Antarctic environment.

(it is called protecting biodiversity) is so important that the leaders of the nations of the world met together in Brazil in 1992 to agree to take steps to protect all life on earth. The polar regions are just as important as the Amazon rainforest, even though there are fewer different animals and plants in the Arctic and Antarctic.

Science in the polar regions

Science is important in the polar regions. It helps us to discover new Arctic resources or, by observing weather patterns in the Antarctic, to understand the climate of the southern hemisphere. Scientists learn about the earth's geological history by studying rocks in Greenland or the Antarctic Peninsula. The ozone 'hole' was discovered in the Antarctic. Finding out about how plants in the Arctic survive freezing temperatures can help us to develop crops that are resistant to frost damage.

Sewage is allowed to be discharged into the Antarctic Ocean, but the amount of human waste is insignificant compared with the waste produced by the four million Adélie penguins that live in the Antarctic.

A young elephant seal displays for a tourist in South Georgia. Experienced guides explain the importance of polar conservation to the tourists.

Scientific research can also help to show us how best to protect the plants and animals in the polar regions. To protect a penguin rookery, for example, we need to know when to avoid going there, so as not to disturb the penguins when they are breeding. We must also learn how much they need to eat, so that we can ensure that fishing boats leave enough krill for the penguins. Scientists can help in deciding which areas should be given special protection so that the animals and plants there have the best chance of survival.

Polar tourism – good or bad?

In recent years, more and more people have been going to the polar regions as tourists. The spectacular scenery of snow and ice and, above all, the accessibility of the wildlife have proved to be a very strong attraction. Polar holidays are expensive, but most people who have taken them think they are well worth while.

The polar regions are easily spoilt by the activities of humans. Governments must enforce the protection laws to preserve the regions' great beauty.

Some people fear that tourists could damage the environment. This is true, but if properly controlled, tourists need have no bad effects. Tour ships in the Antarctic carry experienced guides who explain to the tourists how they should behave so as to avoid damaging the environment or disturbing the wildlife. An advantage of polar tourism is that the returning tourists are often very enthusiastic about the places they have visited, and support their full protection.

The future

In the past, humans have caused much damage in polar regions – whaling in the Antarctic, or oil spills in Alaska, for example. But today we know more about what risks there are, and people in many countries are anxious to avoid further environmental damage. In the Arctic, nations have put in place national laws for protection. In the Antarctic, there is no recognized national authority, but an international agreement has been reached to protect the environment. The laws are in place, but people need to see that their governments enforce the laws to help to preserve some of the most beautiful places on earth.

Protecting the Poles

All the land and coastal seas in the Arctic are under the national control of Russia, the USA, Canada, Greenland and Norway. These countries have made laws to control what people can do in the Arctic.

Although seven nations claim territory in the Antarctic, there is no accepted national authority. Realizing the problems this could cause, the nations active in the Antarctic got together in 1959 and agreed the Antarctic Treaty. This guaranteed that Antarctica would be used for peaceful purposes only, and that there should be complete freedom of scientific research.

Rules for protecting Antarctic animals and plants were introduced as part of the Treaty, and special areas were set aside for extra protection. Waste disposal was regulated and anyone wanting to do anything like build a new research station had to make a careful study of how this might affect the environment. Then they would do it so as to cause as little disturbance as possible.

In 1990, all these rules were revised and some new ones were introduced into what was called the Protocol to the Antarctic Treaty. The Protocol provides a set of rules for the protection of the Antarctic environment. An important new rule was a complete ban on mining in the Antarctic.

Antarctica now has a very strict set of regulations to protect its environment, including all the animals and plants that live there, from the big seals to the tiny mosses. If people observe these rules, Antarctica will be saved for people to enjoy long into the future.

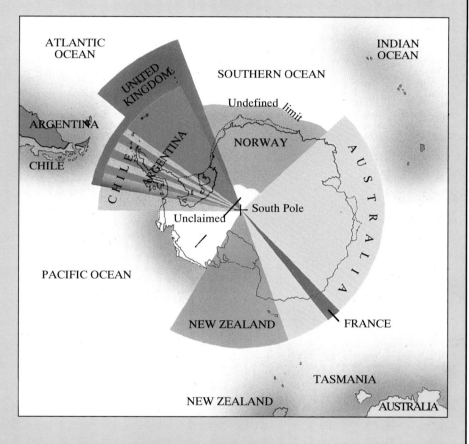

Map showing the territorial claims of seven nations in the Antarctic.

GLOSSARY

Amphibians Cold-blooded animals that live on land and in water, such as frogs and toads.

Atmosphere The air around the earth.

Axis An imaginary line, from the North to the South Pole, around which the earth turns.

Blubber A layer of fat beneath the skin of whales and seals.

Climate The weather conditions of a country.

Colonize To move into a place and start to live there, often pushing out the original inhabitants. Humans, plants or animals can colonize an area.

Commercial hunting Killing a lot of animals and selling their fur, meat or oil to make a profit.

Compass An instrument which points to the magnetic North Pole and so can help you to find your way.

Constellation A group of stars.

Continent A very large land mass.

Equator An imaginary line around the earth, halfway between the North and South Poles.

Fibre-pile A soft, light clothing material which traps a lot of air so that it is a good insulator.

Floes Large sheets of floating ice.

Frostbite Injury caused by the skin and flesh freezing. The fingers, nose, ears and toes are the places where it usually occurs.

Glacier A mass of ice which moves very slowly down a mountain.

Iceberg A huge piece of ice that floats in the sea. You can see only a part of it because most of it is under water.

Ice-cap The mass of ice that permanently covers the land in polar regions.

Ice-shelf A great sheet of floating ice that is attached to the ice covering the land.

Insulator Something which prevents the escape of heat, such as a layer of air trapped in fur or clothing, or blubber.

Latitude The distance, measured in degrees on a map, of a place north or south of the equator.

Lush Thick, green and plentiful.

Pack ice Large pieces of floating ice formed by the surface of the sea freezing. They are all packed together and form floes.

Permafrost Ground that remains frozen throughout the year.

Plankton Small animals and plants drifting near the surface of the sea.

Pollution Substances released into the environment that upset the balance of nature.

Radiation Energy transmitted (given off) as rays, such as heat and light.

Reptiles A group of cold-blooded animals that includes snakes, crocodiles and lizards.

Reserve A store of something you can use if needed. It also means an area set aside for a special purpose.

Rookery A large group of breeding penguins and seals.

Survey To make and record careful measurements.

Synthetic Made artificially.

Tabular iceberg A very large iceberg with a flat top, like a table.

Temperate Moderate or mild in temperature.

Tree line The northern limit where full-sized trees will grow. It is also the highest limit on a mountain where trees grow.

Tropical forests Forests that grow where the climate is hot and damp.

Tropics Two imaginary lines running around the earth to the north and south of the equator. The word 'tropics' also refers to the hot regions near or between these lines.

Tundra The treeless plains in Arctic regions.

Vegetation Plants.

BOOKS TO READ AND FURTHER INFORMATION

Antarctica by Norman Farmer (Batsford, 1993)
How to Survive at the North Pole by Anita Ganeri (Simon & Schuster, 1994)
Peary Reaches the North Pole by Gordon Charleston (Zoe Books, 1993)
Polar Lands by Norman Barrett (Watts, 1989)
Robert Scott in the Antarctic by Philip Sauvain (Zoe Books, 1993)
Understanding the Polar Lands by Lawrence Williams (Evans Brothers, 1990)

It is well worth looking for videos on the polar regions – your library may have some for you to borrow. Ask for the following titles:

Bellamy on Top of the World (Yorkshire TV)
Kingdom of the Ice Bear (BBC)
Life in the Freezer (BBC)

If you want to know more about conservation in polar regions, then write to the following organizations:

Friends of the Earth, 26–28 Underwood Street, London N1 7JQ.
Greenpeace, 30–31 Islington Green, London N1 8XE.
Worldwide Fund for Nature, Panda House, Weyside Park, Godalming, Surrey GU7 1XR.

Picture acknowledgements
Bryan and Cherry Alexander Photography/Rich Kirchner 4(lower), 10(top), 11, /H. Reinhard 22, 25, /David Rootes 26, 27, 29, 31(both), /H. Reinhard 32, /Paul Drummond *title page*, 34, /Ian Cumming 41, 44(top). Mary Evans 37, 38, 39. Natural History Photographic Agency/Hellio and Van Ingren 14(lower), /John Shaw 16, /John Shaw 19, /Bryan and Cherry Alexander 30, 33, /R. Thwaites 40, /Rich Kirchner 43(lower). Still Pictures/Mauri Rautkari 5, /J.J. Alcalay 7(lower), /H. Rappl 8, /Klein-Hubert 10(lower), /Nigel Bonner 12, /Thierry Thomas 13, /H. Rappl 14, 15, /Seitre 17, /Klein-Hubert 18, /Guinet Christope 20, /J.P. Sylvestre 21(top), /Francois Pierrel 21(lower), /Al Grillo 23, /Al Grillo 24, /Inigo Everson 28, /Mimsy Moller 35, /Al Grillo 42, /Cassandra Phillips 43(top), /Thierry Thomas 44(lower). Tony Stone/Terence Harding cover.
Maps and diagrams on pages 4, 6, 7, 9, 12, 19, 23, 28, 29, 36, 38, 45 by Peter Bull.

INDEX